THE WORLD OF OCEAN ANIMALS
SEA LIONS

by Mari Schuh

T0010165

pogo

Ideas for Parents and Teachers

Pogo Books let children practice reading informational text while introducing them to nonfiction features such as headings, labels, sidebars, maps, and diagrams, as well as a table of contents, glossary, and index.

Carefully leveled text with a strong photo match offers early fluent readers the support they need to succeed.

Before Reading

- "Walk" through the book and point out the various nonfiction features. Ask the student what purpose each feature serves.
- Look at the glossary together. Read and discuss the words.

Read the Book

- Have the child read the book independently.
- Invite him or her to list questions that arise from reading.

After Reading

- Discuss the child's questions. Talk about how he or she might find answers to those questions.
- Prompt the child to think more. Ask: What did you know about sea lions before reading this book? What more would you like to learn?

Pogo Books are published by Jump!
5357 Penn Avenue South
Minneapolis, MN 55419
www.jumplibrary.com

Library of Congress Cataloging-in-Publication Data

Names: Schuh, Mari C., 1975- author.
Title: Sea lions / by Mari Schuh.
Description: Minneapolis: Jump!, Inc., [2022]
Series: The world of ocean animals
Includes index. | Audience: Ages 7-10
Identifiers: LCCN 2021000235 (print)
LCCN 2021000236 (ebook)
ISBN 9781636900698 (hardcover)
ISBN 9781636900704 (paperback)
ISBN 9781636900711 (ebook)
Subjects: LCSH: Sea lions—Juvenile literature.
Classification: LCC QL737.P63 S345 2022 (print)
LCC QL737.P63 (ebook) | DDC 599.79/75—dc23
LC record available at https://lccn.loc.gov/2021000235
LC ebook record available at https://lccn.loc.gov/2021000236

Editor: Jenna Gleisner
Designer: Michelle Sonnek

Photo Credits: Eric Isselee/Shutterstock, cover; Wonderly Imaging/Shutterstock, 1; Diego Grandi/Shutterstock, 3; Steve Allen/Shutterstock, 4; Gerald Corsi/iStock, 5; Rob Atherton/Shutterstock, 6-7; Michael Rucker/imageBROKER/SuperStock, 8-9; Juergen Freund/Alamy, 10; Minden Pictures/SuperStock, 11; wildestanimal/Shutterstock, 12-13; Marek Poplawski/Shutterstock, 14; Alexander Machulskiy/Shutterstock, 14-15; neil bowman/iStock, 16-17; Tui De Roy/Minden Pictures/SuperStock, 18; Design Pics Inc/Alamy, 19; Leonardo Gonzalez/Shutterstock, 20-21; volkova natalia/Shutterstock, 23.

Printed in the United States of America at Corporate Graphics in North Mankato, Minnesota.

TABLE OF CONTENTS

CHAPTER 1
Land and Sea..........................4

CHAPTER 2
Loud and Strong.......................10

CHAPTER 3
Sea Lion Pups.........................18

ACTIVITIES & TOOLS
Try This!.............................22
Glossary..............................23
Index.................................24
To Learn More.........................24

LAND AND SEA

A **colony** of sea lions rests on a sandy beach. Their short brown hair shines in the sun. Layers of **blubber** keep them warm. But the sun provides even more warmth.

There are six sea lion **species**. Steller sea lions are the largest. Males are much bigger than females. They can be 11 feet (3.4 meters) long. They can weigh up to 2,500 pounds (1,134 kilograms)!

Steller sea lions

California
sea lions

Most sea lion species live in and
near the Pacific Ocean. They hunt
in the water. They rest, **mate**, and
give birth on land.

TAKE A LOOK!

The California sea lion is the most well-known sea lion species. Take a look at where it lives!

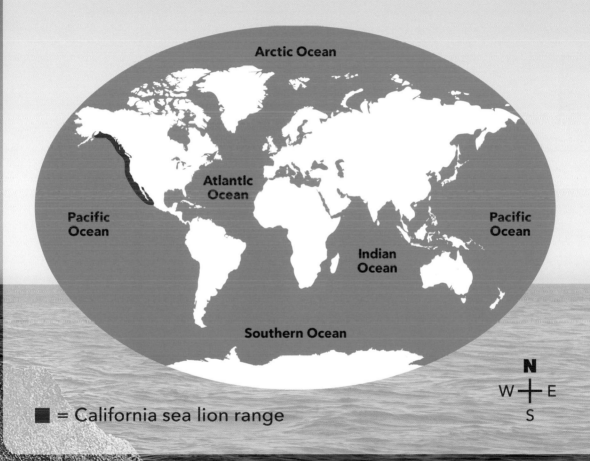

Arctic Ocean

Atlantic Ocean

Pacific Ocean

Pacific Ocean

Indian Ocean

Southern Ocean

■ = California sea lion range

Though they are large, sea lions can move on land. How? They turn their hind flippers forward. They use all four flippers to walk. They can even climb!

TAKE A LOOK!

What are a sea lion's body parts called? Take a look!

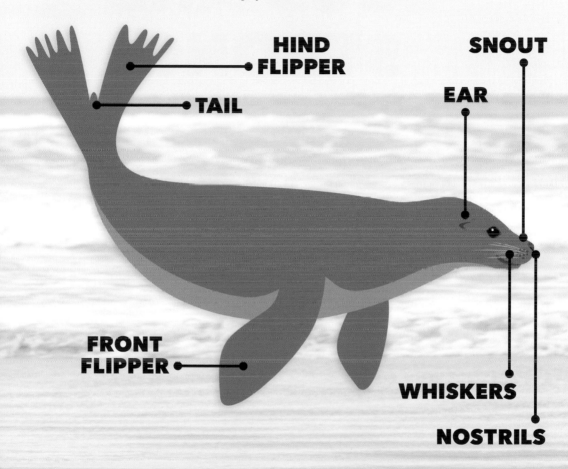

HIND FLIPPER

SNOUT

EAR

TAIL

FRONT FLIPPER

WHISKERS

NOSTRILS

CHAPTER 2

LOUD AND STRONG

Sea lions are strong, fast swimmers. They can swim up to 30 miles (48 kilometers) per hour. They swim quickly to play, find food, and escape **predators**.

Orcas and sharks hunt sea lions. How do sea lions stay safe? Their **flexible** bodies help them twist and turn as they swim away. They can also use their teeth to attack predators.

Sea lions are also good divers.
They can hold their breath for
up to 20 minutes! They dive deep
in the ocean to look for food.
Sea lions hunt fish, octopuses,
and squid.

DID YOU KNOW?

Sea lions often swallow their
prey whole. Sometimes they
toss their food up in the air.
Then they eat it in one big gulp.

Sea lions also eat penguins and **crustaceans**, such as crabs. Their whiskers help them **sense** their prey's movement in the water.

crab

◄·····whiskers

mane

Sea lions are noisy and loud. They bark, honk, and roar. This is how they **communicate** in their colony. When it's time to mate, males are very noisy. This helps them claim and defend their **territories**.

DID YOU KNOW?

Sea lions roar, much like lions. Many male sea lions also have manes. This is how sea lions got their name.

SEA LION PUPS

Females and their **pups** have their own sounds. These help them find each other. Sea lions are **mammals**. Females usually give birth to one pup a year. Pups are born on land. Their coats are smooth and silky.

pup

Pups drink their mothers' milk. Mothers also find food for their pups.

After just a few weeks, pups can swim. As they grow, they get ready for life in the ocean. They learn how to hunt. Pups also learn how to escape predators. After about one year, many pups are ready to live on their own.

DID YOU KNOW?

Pollution and **climate change** harm sea lions. Fishing nets do, too. Sea lions can get caught in them. People work to keep the ocean clean. How can you help keep sea lions safe?

ACTIVITIES & TOOLS

TRY THIS!

TEXTURE GUESSING GAME

Sea lions have short, coarse hair. Sea lion pups are born with smooth, silky coats. Explore the different ways items feel with this fun guessing game.

What You Need:
- several items that have different textures, such as marbles, leaves, rocks, rubber bands, sandpaper, cloth or fabrics, silk flowers, ribbons, or feathers
- a large box
- a few friends

① Gather several items that have different textures. Put all the items in a large box.

② Put your hand in the box. Pick up one item while keeping your hand in the box. Carefully feel the item. Do not show the item to your friends.

③ Describe how the item feels. Is it hard or soft? Is it smooth or rough? Maybe it's fluffy or bumpy. What is the item used for?

④ Have your friends guess what the item is. The friend who guesses correctly is the next person to feel an item in the box.

GLOSSARY

blubber: A thick layer of fat under the skin of some ocean animals.

climate change: Changes in Earth's weather and climate over time.

colony: A group of sea lions on land.

communicate: To share information, ideas, or feelings with another.

crustaceans: Types of ocean animals that have outer skeletons, such as lobsters, crabs, and shrimp.

flexible: Able to bend or move easily.

mammals: Warm-blooded animals that give birth to live young, which drink milk from their mothers.

mate: To join together to produce young.

pollution: Harmful materials that damage or contaminate the air, water, or soil.

predators: Animals that hunt other animals for food.

prey: Animals that are hunted by other animals for food.

pups: Young sea lions.

sense: To feel or become aware of something.

species: One of the groups into which similar animals and plants are divided.

territories: Areas that animals claim and defend.

INDEX

blubber 4

body parts 9

California sea lions 7

climate change 20

colony 4, 17

communicate 17

dive 13

females 5, 18

flippers 8, 9

hair 4

hunt 6, 11, 13, 20

males 5, 17

mammals 18

mate 6, 17

Pacific Ocean 6, 7

pollution 20

predators 10, 11, 20

prey 13, 14

pups 18, 19, 20

species 5, 6, 7

Steller sea lions 5

swim 10, 11, 20

teeth 11

territories 17

walk 8

whiskers 9, 14

TO LEARN MORE

Finding more information is as easy as 1, 2, 3.

1. Go to www.factsurfer.com
2. Enter "sealions" into the search box.
3. Choose your book to see a list of websites.

FACT SURFER